P9-DNM-915

How to Draw
Incredible DISCARD
Aliens
and Cool Space Stuff

BARRON'S

Created and produced by Green Android Ltd

Illustrated by Fiona Gowen

First edition for North America
published in 2015 by
Barron's Educational Series, Inc.

Copyright © Green Android Ltd 2014

Green Android Ltd
49 Beaumont Court
Upper Clapton Road
London E5 8BG
United Kingdom
www.greenandroid.co.uk

All inquiries should be addressed to:
Barron's Educational Series, Inc.
250 Wireless Boulevard
Hauppauge, NY 11788
www.barronseduc.com

ISBN: 978-1-4380-0584-3

Date of Manufacture: January 2015
Manufactured by:
Toppan Leefung Printing Co., Ltd.,
Dongguan, China

Printed in China
9 8 7 6 5 4 3 2 1

All rights reserved.
No part of this publication may be reproduced or
distributed in any form or by any means without
the written permission of the copyright owner.

Contents

R0443521447

4 Super Rockets

6 Mighty Shuttle

8 Incredible Satellites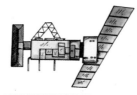

10 Moon Landing

12 Amazing Rovers

14 Space Stations

16 Fantastic Telescopes

18 Cool Astronauts

20 The Solar System

22 Rocks in Space

24 UFOs

26 Mad Martians

28 Incredible Aliens

30 Traveling in the Future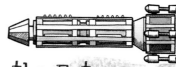

Page 32 has an index of everything to draw in this book.

How to Draw

Super Rockets

Every astronaut uses a rocket to travel into outer space. There are many different types of rockets, but they all have a similar shape.

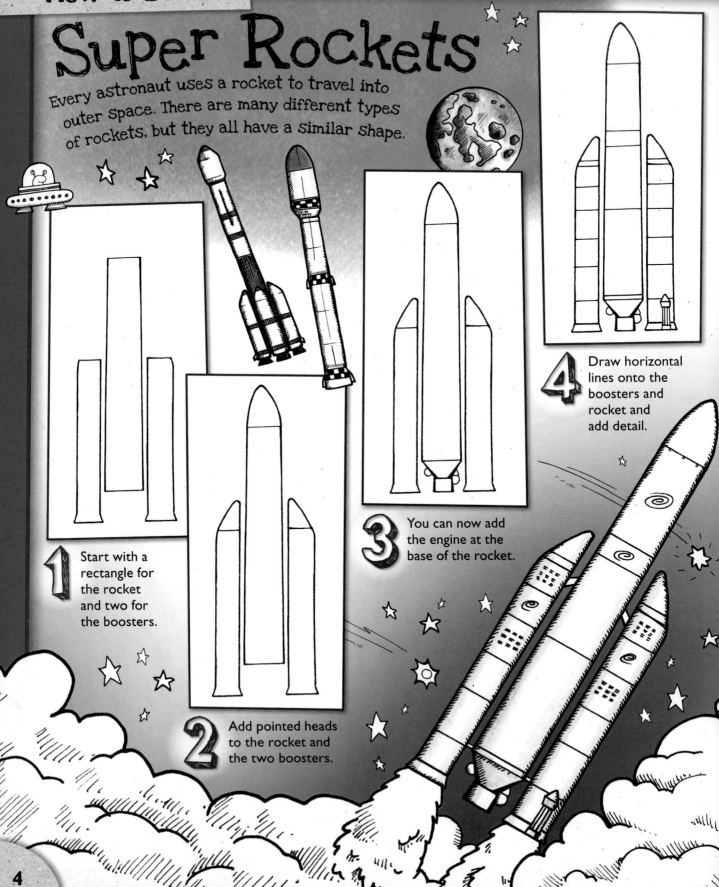

1 Start with a rectangle for the rocket and two for the boosters.

2 Add pointed heads to the rocket and the two boosters.

3 You can now add the engine at the base of the rocket.

4 Draw horizontal lines onto the boosters and rocket and add detail.

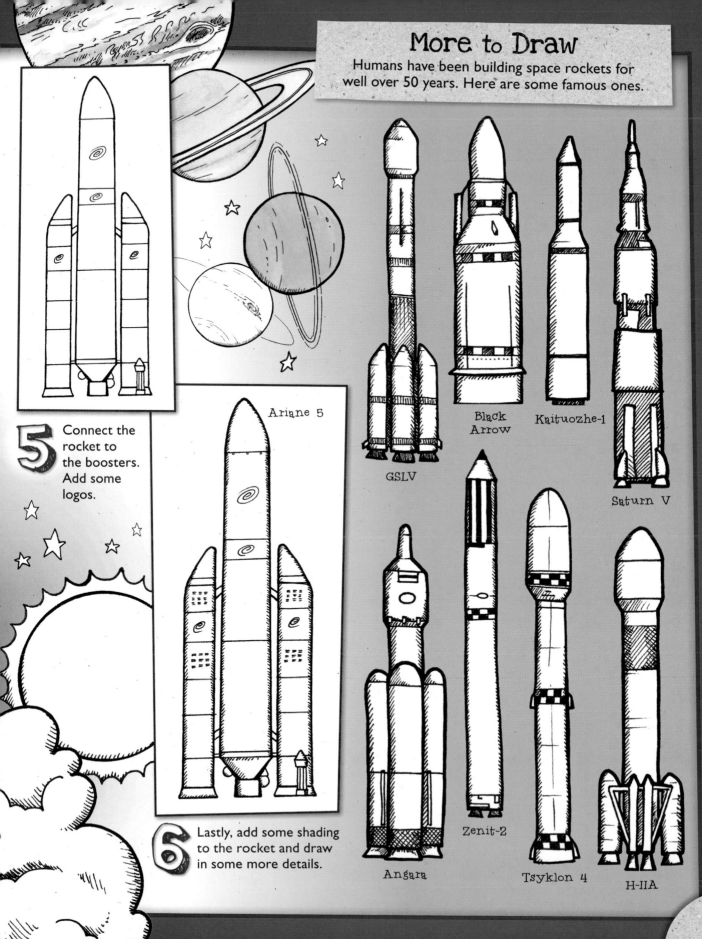

More to Draw

Humans have been building space rockets for well over 50 years. Here are some famous ones.

5 Connect the rocket to the boosters. Add some logos.

Ariane 5

6 Lastly, add some shading to the rocket and draw in some more details.

GSLV

Black Arrow

Kaituozhe-1

Saturn V

Angara

Zenit-2

Tsyklon 4

H-IIA

Mighty Shuttle

The space shuttle is a very well known spacecraft. It was first launched in 1981 and made over 135 missions into outer space during its 30-year career.

1 Start your shuttle picture by drawing the vertical stabilizer.

2 You can now draw the outline of the shuttle and its wings.

3 Add the payload doors on top and the main engines at the back.

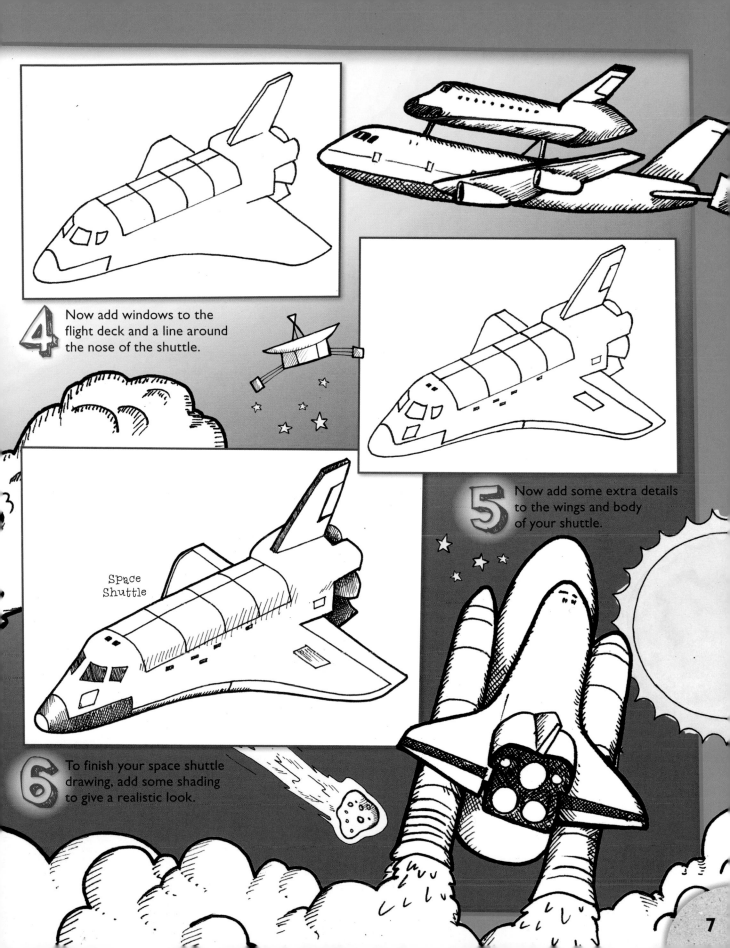

4 Now add windows to the flight deck and a line around the nose of the shuttle.

5 Now add some extra details to the wings and body of your shuttle.

Space Shuttle

6 To finish your space shuttle drawing, add some shading to give a realistic look.

How to Draw
Incredible Satellites

Man-made satellites are machines that are launched into space. Some telephone calls and TV signals are sent all around the world by satellites.

1 Start by drawing the three parts of the body.

2 Now draw an outline for a solar shield at the back and the large solar panels at the front.

3 Add details to the solar shield, the solar panels, and the main body.

4 Draw shapes on the body for instruments and three antennae underneath.

Over 6,600 satellites have been launched into space. They come in all sorts of weird and wonderful shapes.

5 Now draw the large receiving and transmitting antenna onto the top of your satellite.

6 Finally, add details, shadows, and reflections to your satellite to make it realistic.

Ajisai

Galaxy-12

Asterix

ZY-3

Cryosat-2

NOAA 17

Jason-2

Starlette

Zeya

AMC-8

How to Draw

Moon Landing

A lunar module is a small spacecraft that carries astronauts from lunar orbit to the surface of the moon, and then back again to the orbiting command module.

Landing module

1 Start by drawing an outline for the base section of the lunar module.

2 Now you can draw one of the sides onto the body of your lunar module.

3 You can now add the entrance hatch to your lunar module drawing.

4 Add the legs and all of the support struts.

Lunar module

6 Finally, add some shadows and reflections to your lunar module.

5 Now add some details to your drawing, such as the various antennae, instruments, and lights.

Amazing Rovers

Rovers are vehicles used for traveling across the surface of planets and moons. Some are designed to carry passengers, while others work like robots.

1 Start by drawing the wheels and wheel arches of the rover.

2 Now you can draw a long horizontal shape to form the base of the vehicle.

3 Add a basic seat structure for the driver and the controls for driving the lunar rover.

4 Add the relay unit at the front of the rover and the collection bags behind the driver's seat.

Some lunar rovers can carry two passengers, while others carry a camera and are controlled remotely.

Apollo 17 lunar rover

Opportunity rover

Apollo 16 lunar rover

Space exploration vehicle

5 Now you can draw on the high-gain antenna, which looks like an open umbrella on a pole.

Apollo 15 lunar rover

Sojourner

Prop-M rover

Lunokhod 1

6 To finish your drawing, add some shaded areas and dark lines to give some extra details.

Chariot lunar rover

Curiosity rover

How to Draw
Space Stations

Space stations are designed to stay in orbit for a long time. Other spacecraft can dock onto the space stations to perform research.

1 Start your space station with a long, thin shape.

2 Now you can add the large solar panels. There should be 16 of these panels.

3 Draw the two radiator panels that maintain temperature on the space station.

4 Now add the main body, which contains the living quarters, equipment room, and laboratory.

More to Draw

Space stations have varied designs,
but they have similar equipment on board.

Skylab

Kosmos 557

Tiangong 2

Almaz

Salyut 6

Salyut 7

Salyut 4

Salyut 1

Mir

5 Now draw the service module and cargo ferry at the end of the main body of the space station.

International
Space Station

6 To finish the drawing, shade some areas darker to give the space station a metallic effect.

Fantastic Telescopes

Nowadays, astronomers use many different types of telescopes to study and discover new things about space.

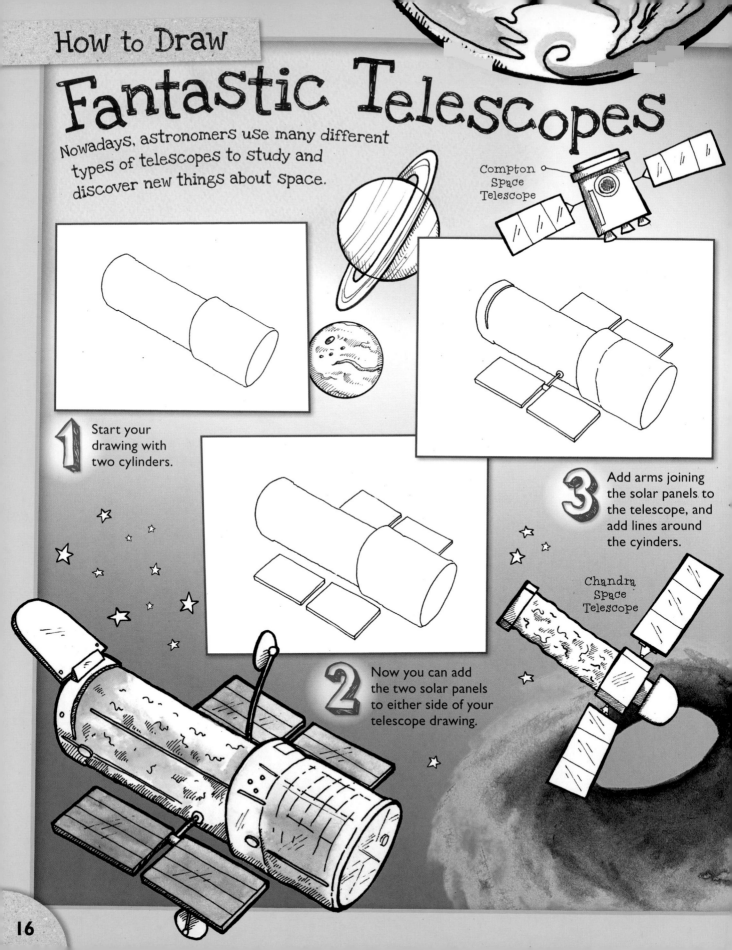

Compton Space Telescope

1 Start your drawing with two cylinders.

2 Now you can add the two solar panels to either side of your telescope drawing.

3 Add arms joining the solar panels to the telescope, and add lines around the cyinders.

Chandra Space Telescope

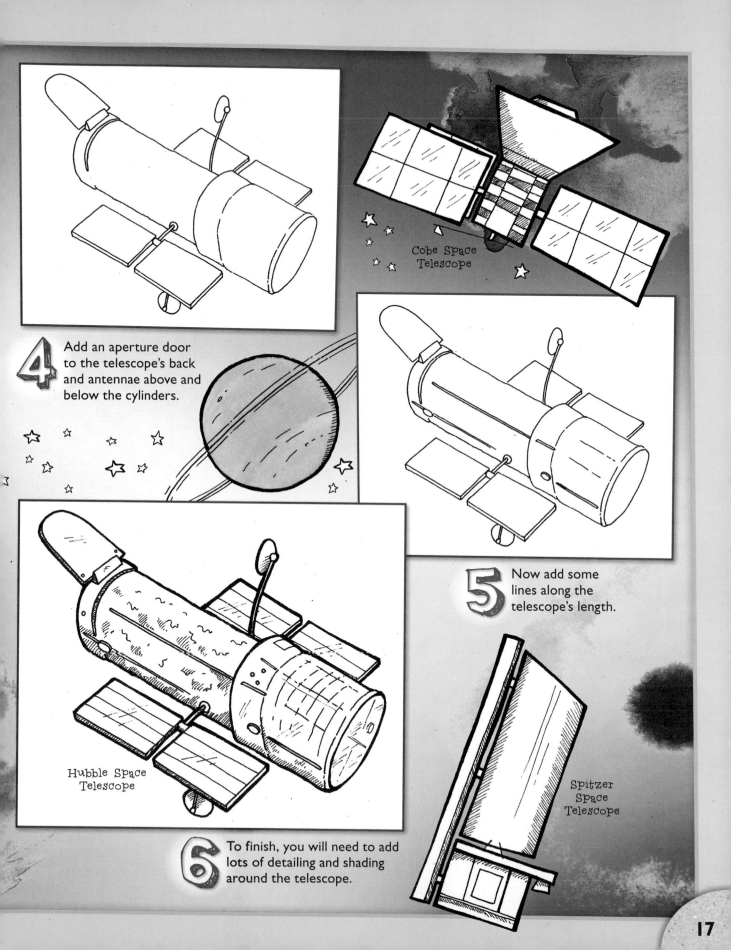

Cobe Space
Telescope

4 Add an aperture door
to the telescope's back
and antennae above and
below the cylinders.

5 Now add some
lines along the
telescope's length.

Hubble Space
Telescope

Spitzer
Space
Telescope

6 To finish, you will need to add
lots of detailing and shading
around the telescope.

How to Draw
Cool Astronauts

Astronauts are among the few people to experience the thrill of blast-off, to see the Earth from outer space, and to float weightlessly in a spacecraft.

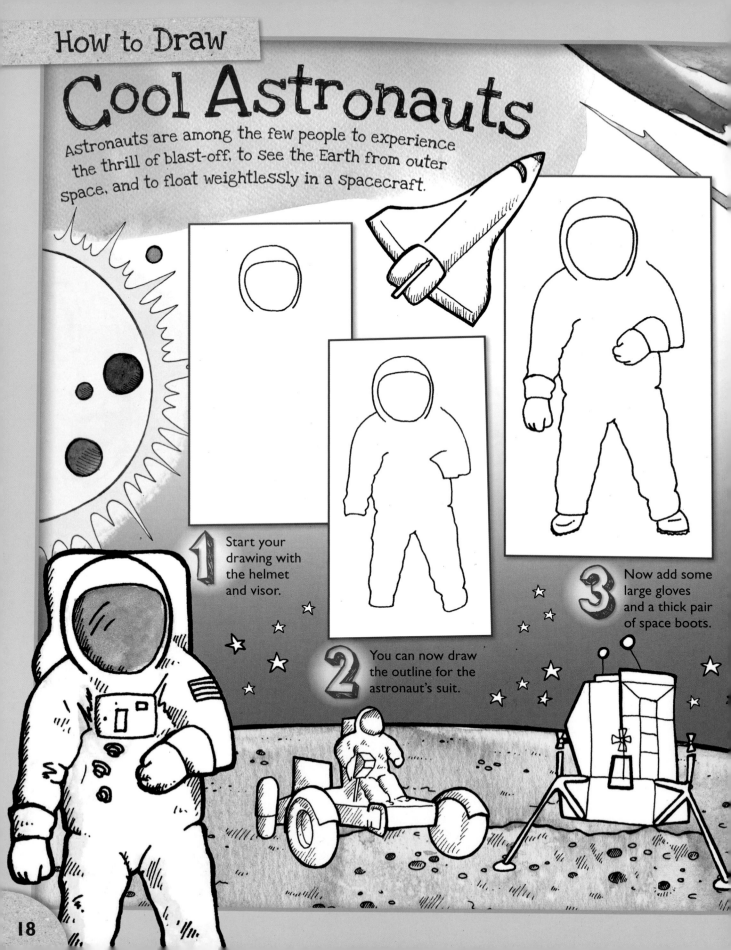

1 Start your drawing with the helmet and visor.

2 You can now draw the outline for the astronaut's suit.

3 Now add some large gloves and a thick pair of space boots.

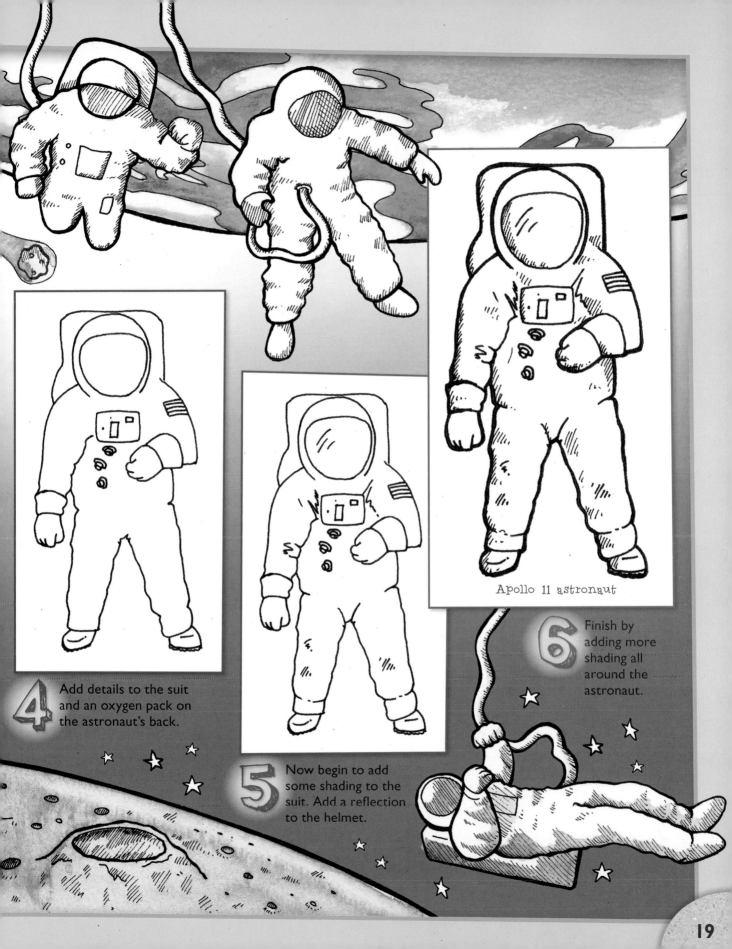

Apollo 11 astronaut

4 Add details to the suit and an oxygen pack on the astronaut's back.

5 Now begin to add some shading to the suit. Add a reflection to the helmet.

6 Finish by adding more shading all around the astronaut.

How to Draw
The Solar System

Our solar system is made up of a large star called the Sun, eight planets, 146 moons, comets, asteroids, space rocks, and dwarf planets, such as Pluto.

Mercury

The Sun

Venus

The Moon

Earth

1 Start your drawing of Earth with a large circle.

Mars

Jupiter

2 You can now begin to draw in some land. This shape represents North America.

3 Add another landmass below North America. This area represents South America.

4 Now add some islands for the Caribbean and some large lakes as shown.

Saturn

Uranus

Neptune

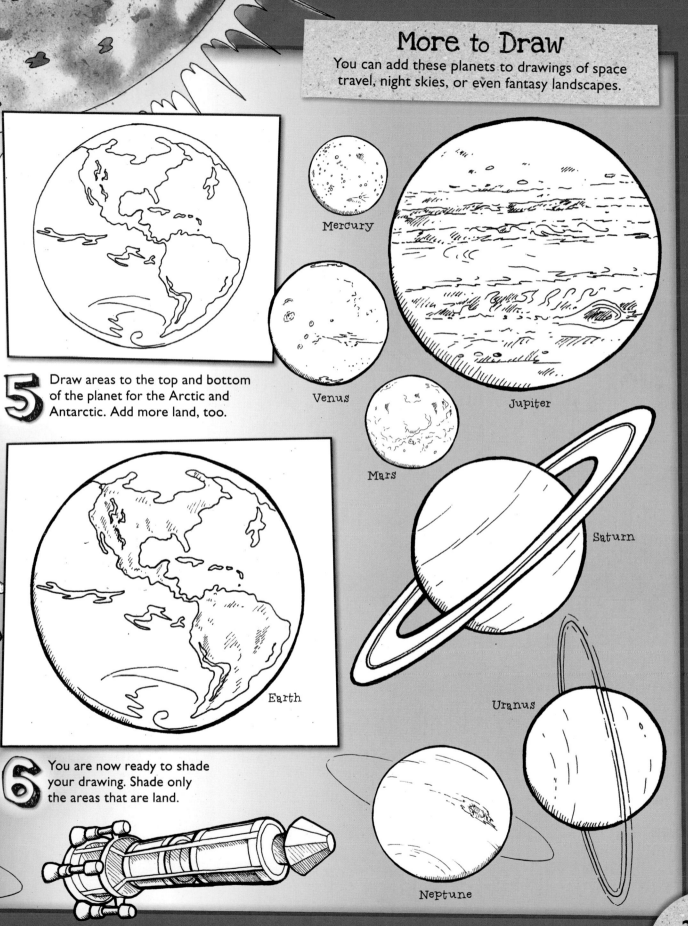

5 Draw areas to the top and bottom of the planet for the Arctic and Antarctic. Add more land, too.

6 You are now ready to shade your drawing. Shade only the areas that are land.

Mercury

Venus

Jupiter

Mars

Earth

Saturn

Uranus

Neptune

How to Draw

Rocks in Space

Asteroids are small, rocky bodies left over from the formation of the planets 4.5 billion years ago. They are sometimes called minor planets.

1 Start the asteroid drawing with a rock shape.

2 Add details to the asteroid with some circles, dots, and some shaded areas.

3 Now draw an outline all the way around your asteroid.

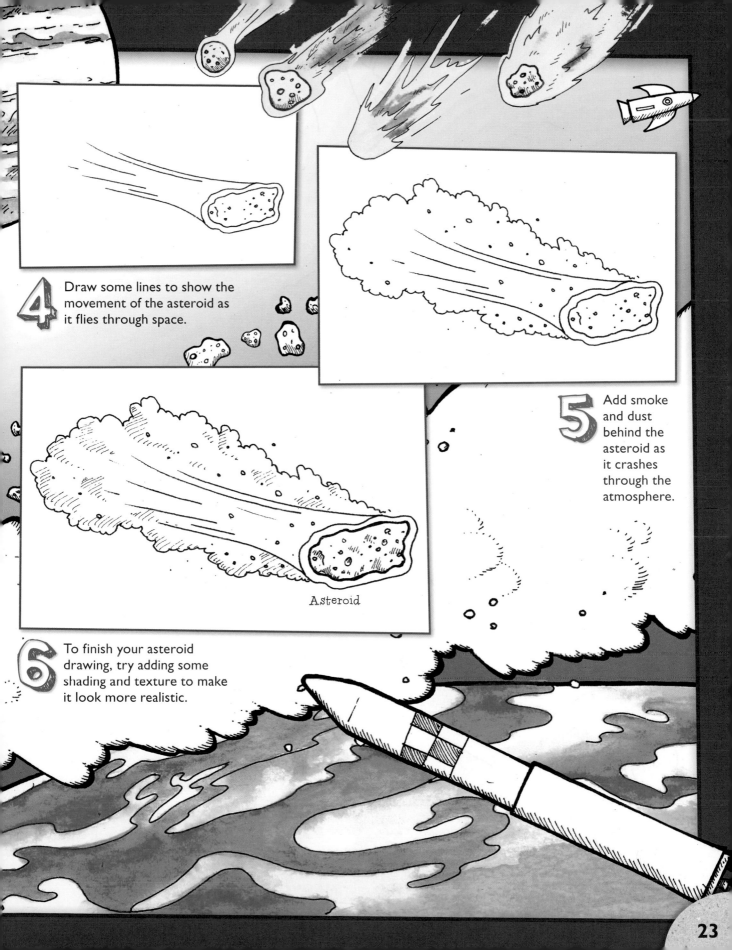

4 Draw some lines to show the movement of the asteroid as it flies through space.

5 Add smoke and dust behind the asteroid as it crashes through the atmosphere.

Asteroid

6 To finish your asteroid drawing, try adding some shading and texture to make it look more realistic.

How to Draw

UFOs

UFOs are unidentified flying objects — no one really knows what they are. Could these objects belong to visitors from another planet?

1 Start by drawing three connecting oval shapes.

2 Draw a curve over the top of the UFO and then add a row of lights underneath.

3 Add a curved shape on top of your UFO with two smaller curves either side of it.

4 Divide the underside of the UFO into four sections. Add a window to each section.

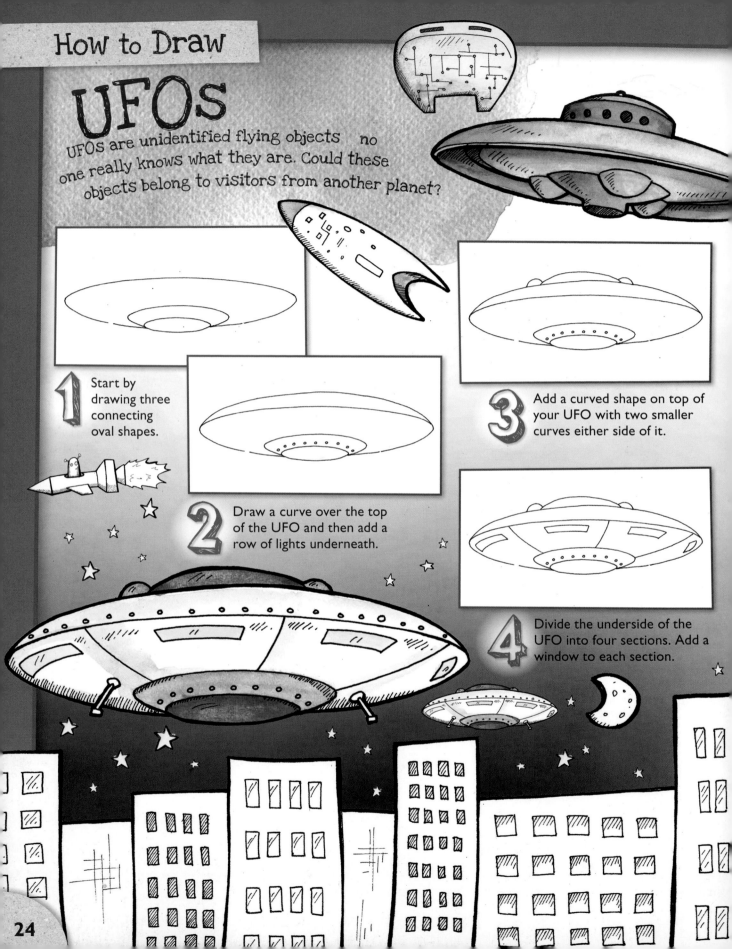

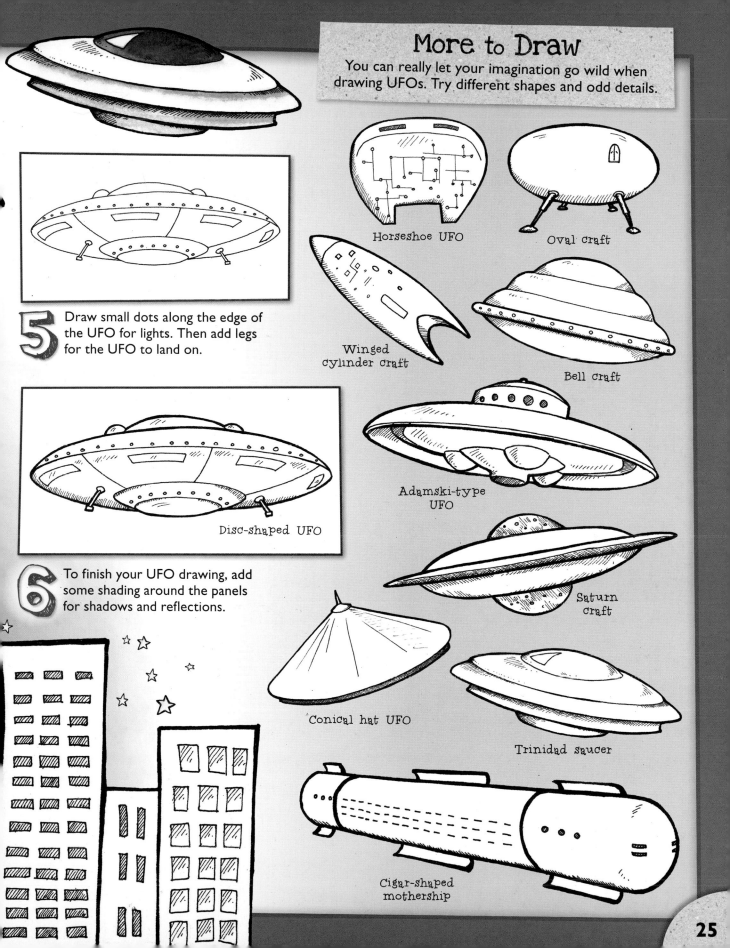

More to Draw

You can really let your imagination go wild when drawing UFOs. Try different shapes and odd details.

5 Draw small dots along the edge of the UFO for lights. Then add legs for the UFO to land on.

Disc-shaped UFO

6 To finish your UFO drawing, add some shading around the panels for shadows and reflections.

Horseshoe UFO

Oval craft

Winged cylinder craft

Bell craft

Adamski-type UFO

Saturn craft

Conical hat UFO

Trinidad saucer

Cigar-shaped mothership

25

How to Draw
Mad Martians

Some people believe that aliens from Mars have already visited Earth. Various reports describe these Martians as having human-like bodies.

1 Start your Martian by drawing a lightbulb-shaped head with a diamond below.

2 Now add the face, the outline of the body, and the shoulders of the Martian's uniform.

3 Add the arms, cuffs, collars, and belt, Give the Martian a large helmet.

Emperor Martian

4 You can now add the Martian's hands and feet to your drawing.

5 Draw a line down the uniform and add a long line of buttons.

6 To finish your drawing, add more details and some shading.

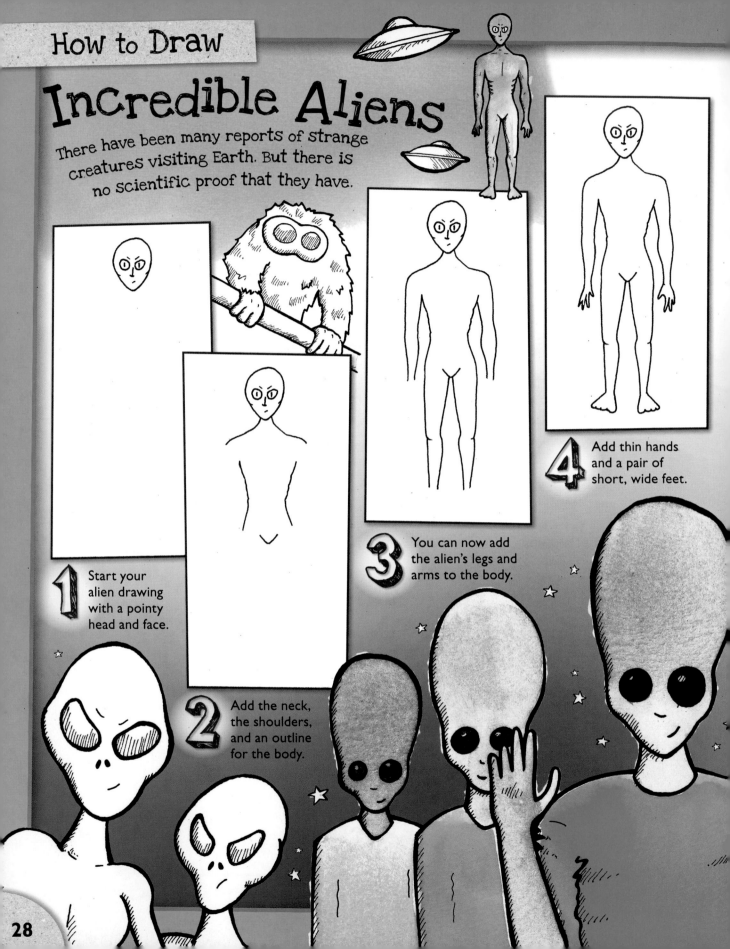

How to Draw

Incredible Aliens

There have been many reports of strange creatures visiting Earth. But there is no scientific proof that they have.

1 Start your alien drawing with a pointy head and face.

2 Add the neck, the shoulders, and an outline for the body.

3 You can now add the alien's legs and arms to the body.

4 Add thin hands and a pair of short, wide feet.

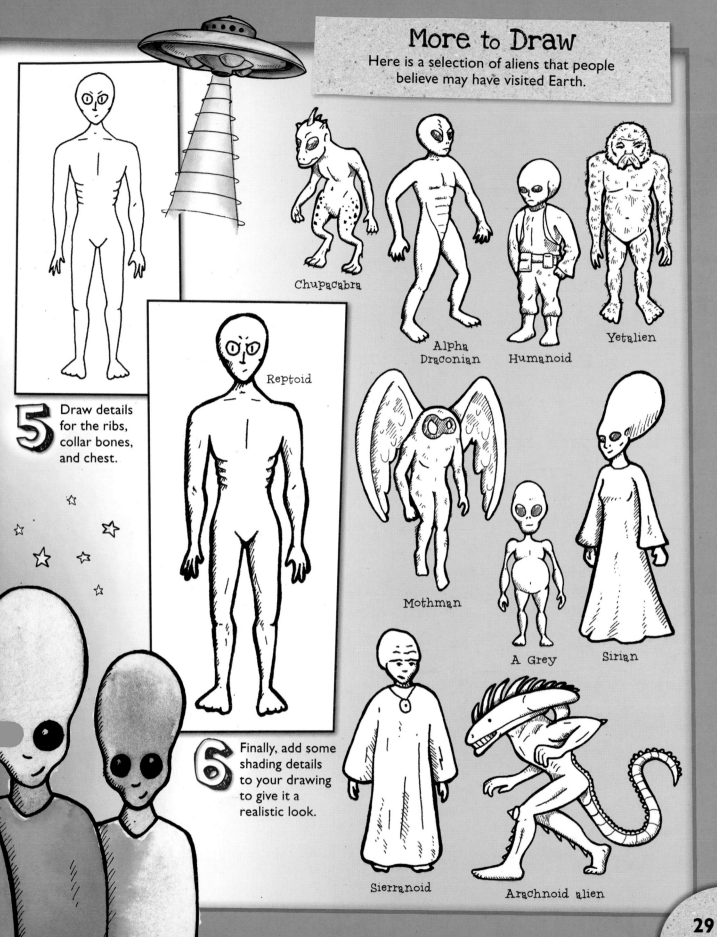

5 Draw details for the ribs, collar bones, and chest.

Reptoid

6 Finally, add some shading details to your drawing to give it a realistic look.

Chupacabra

Alpha Draconian

Humanoid

Yetalien

Mothman

A Grey

Sirian

Sierranoid

Arachnoid alien

Traveling in the Future

We have now been traveling into space for over 50 years. Who knows what type of spacecraft and vehicles will be developed in another 50 years!

1 Start your deep spacecraft picture by drawing two rectangles.

2 Now you can draw three powerful rocket boosters onto the square.

3 Add some panels and struts to the rectangle part of your spacecraft.

4 Now join the rectangles together. Add a pointed nose to the front of your spacecraft.

5 Draw some panels on the pointed nose of the spacecraft and a row of lights along the top.

Deep space craft

6 You can now finish your drawing by shading in the panels to show which areas are in shadow.

Space hotel

Personal spacecraft

Space plane

Skylon

White Knight Two

Space flight vehicle

Strato cruiser

Lynx space craft

Space glider

Index

There are lots of exciting things to draw in this book. Practice your newfound drawing skills by adding some of them to your drawings.

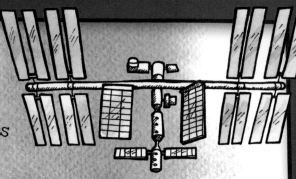

A Grey	29	
Adamski-type UFO	25	
Ajisai	9	
Almaz	15	
Alpha Draconian	29	
AMC-8	9	
Angara	5	
Apollo 11 astronaut	19	
Apollo 15 lunar rover	13	
Apollo 16 lunar rover	13	
Apollo 17 lunar rover	13	
Arachnoid alien	29	
Ariane 5	5	
Asterix	9	
Asteroid	23	
Bell craft	25	
Black Arrow	5	
Chandra Space Telescope	16	
Chariot lunar rover	13	
Chupacabra	29	
Cigar-shaped mothership	25	
Cobe Space Telescope	17	
Compton Space Telescope	16	
Conical hat UFO	25	
Cryosat-2	9	
Curiosity rover	13	
Deep space craft	31	
Disc-shaped UFO	25	
Earth	20-21	
Emperor Martian	27	
Galaxy-12	9	
GSLV	5	
H-IIA	5	
Horseshoe UFO	25	
Hubble Space Telescope	17	
Humanoid	29	
International Space Station	15	
Jason-2	9	
Jupiter	20-21	
Kaituozhe-1	5	
Kosmos 557	15	
Landing module	10	
Lunar module	11	
Lunokhod 1	13	
Lynx space craft	31	
Mars	20-21	
Mercury	20-21	
Mir	15	
Mothman	29	
Neptune	20-21	
NOAA 17	9	
Opportunity rover	13	
Oval craft	25	
Personal spacecraft	31	
Prop-M rover	13	
Reptoid	29	
Salyut 1	15	
Salyut 4	15	
Salyut 6	15	
Salyut 7	15	
Saturn	20-21	
Saturn craft	25	
Saturn V	5	
Sierranoid	29	
Sirian	29	
Skylab	15	
Skylon	31	
Sojourner	13	
Space exploration vehicle	13	
Space flight vehicle	31	
Space glider	31	
Space hotel	31	
Space plane	31	
Space Shuttle	7	
Spitzer Space Telescope	17	
Starlette	9	
Strato cruiser	31	
The Moon	20	
The Sun	20	
Tiangong 2	15	
Trinidad saucer	25	
Tsyklon 4	5	
Uranus	20-21	
Venus	20-21	
White Knight Two	31	
Winged cylinder craft	25	
Yetalien	29	
Zenit-2	5	
Zeya	9	
ZY-3	9	

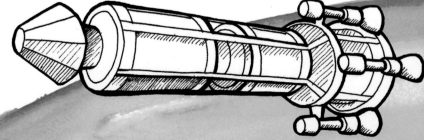